JACK'S SACK

Written by Susan Akass

Illustrated by Philippe Dupasquier

Rigby

The night was cold,
the night was black,
when
   two
      robbers
         crept

to the tumbledown shack.

They were
Fat-Cat Charlie
and
Mean-Eyed Jack.

WANTED

Fat-Cat Charlie

WANTED

Mean-Eyed Jack

They carried their gold
in a great big sack.

"This gold is heavy!"
cried Mean-Eyed Jack.
He dropped the sack,

crack!

and the shack went *crack!*

Down came the front wall,
down came the back,
and it hit them both
with a mighty whack!

"Help!" cried Charlie.
"Help!" cried Jack.

"The police have found us!
We're under attack!"

They didn't stop.
They didn't look back.

They ran from the shack
without their sack!

"Hello, Charlie.
Hello, Jack."